His Treasure

Gems of Love from Your King

Sheri Rose Shepherd

**TYNDALE
MOMENTUM**

*An Imprint of
Tyndale House Publishers, Inc.*

Visit Tyndale online at www.tyndale.com.

Visit Tyndale Momentum online at www.tyndalemomentum.com.

Visit Sheri Rose Shepherd at biblelifecoaching.com.

TYNDALE is a registered trademark of Tyndale House Publishers, Inc.
Tyndale Momentum and the Tyndale Momentum logo are trademarks
of Tyndale House Publishers, Inc. Tyndale Momentum is an imprint
of Tyndale House Publishers, Inc.

His Treasure: Gems of Love from Your King

Designed by Jennifer Ghionzoli

Published in association with the Loyal Arts Literary Agency, PO Box 1414,
Bend, OR 97709.

Scripture quotations are taken from the *Holy Bible*, New Living Translation,
copyright © 1996, 2004, 2007, 2013 by Tyndale House Foundation. Used
by permission of Tyndale House Publishers, Inc., Carol Stream, Illinois
60188. All rights reserved.

Scripture quotations marked NIV are taken from the Holy Bible, *New
International Version,*® *NIV.*® Copyright © 1973, 1978, 1984, 2011
by Biblica, Inc.™ (Some quotations may be from the 1984 edition.)
Used by permission of Zondervan. All rights reserved worldwide.
www.zondervan.com.

Scripture quotations marked NKJV are taken from the New King James
Version.® Copyright © 1982 by Thomas Nelson, Inc. Used by permission.
All rights reserved.

ISBN 978-1-4143-6693-7

Printed in China

18 17 16 15 14 13
6   5   4   3   2   1

*I want to dedicate this book to the four women
who prayed me into the Kingdom of God:*

MY BEAUTIFUL MOTHER-IN-LOVE,
Janice Joy Shepherd

MY ANOINTED SPIRITUAL MOTHER,
Emilie Pyle

MY LOVING STEPMOTHER,
Susie Goodman

MY PRECIOUS MOTHER,
Carole Goodman

Contents

Introduction

Out of all the peoples on the face of the earth, the LORD has chosen you to be his treasured possession.

DEUTERONOMY 14:2, NIV

You are His treasure. . . . How you feel about yourself will never change God's unconditional love for you.

Your heavenly Father's deep desire is to be close to you, but He will not force His way into your heart. He will wait patiently for you to invite Him to walk with you together as Father and daughter.

Get ready to breathe in the Father's never-ending love for you and to discover His treasures of truth as you have a whole new encounter with your King. May every word on the following pages go down deep, and may you never forget the riches you have in Christ and how much you are loved by Him!

Love,
Your sister in Christ, Sheri Rose

My Beloved Daughter,

My love for you cannot be taken away. What you are searching for is found in My heavenly arms. I can promise you this: if you will seek Me first above all others, you will find that I am all you need to feel safe and secure. My love for you is everlasting and effortless because you are My daughter. My deepest desire is to be close to you, but I will not force My way into your heart. I will wait patiently for you to invite Me in, and when you're ready, we will walk together as Father and daughter every day for the rest of your life—until the day I see your face in heaven. For now, breathe in My never-ending love for you and smile, knowing you are My treasure.

Love,
Your loving Father

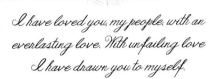

I have loved you, my people, with an everlasting love. With unfailing love I have drawn you to myself.

JEREMIAH 31:3

TREASURE OF TRUTH

How you feel about yourself will never change God's unconditional love for you.

3

Weeping may
last through the night,
but joy comes with
the morning.

PSALM 30:5

His Encouragement

My Beloved Daughter,

I know you wonder where I am in the middle of your pain. Although you can't see Me, My eyes are always on you, and I see every tear that has ever rolled off your precious face. My Father's heart breaks as I look for ways to remind you that My comfort is only a whisper away. Your feelings will always deceive you, which is why I gave you My Holy Spirit. The next time your heart doubts Me, pray and reflect on the last time you were sure I had forsaken you. Remember that I was there all along, working out what you could not see in your moment of mourning. I have always been with you; I was there when you cried your first tear, and I will be there to catch your last tear on earth. This weeping will not last, My love, but it will lead you back to Me, where your joy, hope, and love will once again be restored as you soak in My presence.

Love,
Your tender, loving God

TREASURE OF TRUTH

Our God does not waste pain . . . but He does
wipe away every tear.

His plan begins in your heart before it is displayed in your life.

Wherever your treasure is, there the desires
of your heart will also be.

LUKE 12:34

6

His Plan

My Child,

I know you have a passion inside of you to do something bigger than yourself. My plan for your life has already been put into motion; however, you will remain in a holding pattern until I alone am enough for you. Because I love you, My ultimate plan for you will begin to unfold only when I have your full adoration and attention. Wherever your treasure is and whatever you value most will direct your heart and ultimately your destiny.

If your desire is to see what your faith and My power can conquer through your life, you must give up anything that feeds your flesh more than your spirit. I am a holy God, and I can give you only as much as you are willing to lay down. If you will lose your life, you will find it. It is impossible for you to outgive Me because I am a generous God who can and will reward you with far greater life than you could ever give yourself.

Love,
Your King of wonders

My Beloved Child,

The battle is never easy; however, the victory is ever-lasting if it is fought for My glory in My strength. Don't give up your faith when you're worn out from the struggles of life. I have an endless supply of grace to get you through the pain, persecution, and problems this life brings. You will lose only if you forget what you're fighting for. Yes, you will have many days when the blows of the enemy will leave you feeling as if you have been knocked out. However, victory is not measured by how you feel or what you win or lose; it is measured by your witness in the midst of warfare that wins souls for My Kingdom. Your strength will be renewed when you focus on fighting for what is right in My sight. Now is not the time to give in or give up; rather, it is time to get on your knees and let Me reveal to you what is worth fighting for!

Love,
Your faithful Father who fights for you

For the LORD your God is going with you! He will fight for you against your enemies, and he will give you victory!

DEUTERONOMY 20:4

TREASURE OF TRUTH

It is not who you are fighting against that matters; it is what you are fighting for!

His Request

My Beautiful Daughter,

I am the King of kings and the lover of your soul, and there is no one who can give you what I can. I have just one request: take time to connect your heart to Mine in song, in Scripture, in prayer, in praise, and in deed. You will find Me when you search for Me with all your heart. You will experience Me in a whole new way when you choose to love Me with all your heart and all your soul and all your mind. I will no longer seem invisible to you when you seek to make Me visible. When you live fully to gain My attention, you will find My adoration is enough for you, and no one will be able to come between us again. Now, My love, ask Me and I will show you that I truly am all you'll ever need!

Love,
The King who satisfies

You must love the LORD your God with all your heart, all your soul, all your strength, and all your mind.

LUKE 10:27

TREASURE OF TRUTH

You won't know God is all you need until God is all you wholeheartedly seek and want.

"My grace is all you need.
My power works best in weakness."
So now I am glad to boast about
my weaknesses, so that the power
of Christ can work through me.

2 CORINTHIANS 12:9

12

His Strength

My Precious Child,

I want you to experience the benefits and blessings of being Mine. I want you to know the power of grace that only I can give you. You won't discover who I really am in your own strength. You can conquer and accomplish much on your own, but you will never know the joy of work that makes an everlasting difference until you come to the end of yourself. It is in your weakest moments that My strength will become your strength. Only then will My Holy Spirit, who lives inside of you, rise up. Then you will know that I am with you always. If you will embrace your weaknesses and grab hold of all I am, you will become all you desire to be. Now is the time to let Me do great things in you and through you!

Love,
Your strong and mighty God

TREASURE OF TRUTH

In your weakest moment, you'll experience the benefits of being a child of the King.

My Beloved,

Your faith will soar when you look up to Me and let go of what you see in the natural world. Don't you know by now that I will do the supernatural for you if you will allow Me to? You no longer have to be controlled by your circumstances; you can choose to live fueled by faith in Me, starting today. What you see on this earth may cause you to lose hope, but your trust in Me will free you from fear and doubt. Faith in Me will give you the power to persevere with passion and purpose. I want you to learn that what I say and do can never be shaken or taken without your permission. Now breathe in My presence, My child, and choose to never again doubt in the darkness what you know to be true in the light of My truth.

Love,
Your faithful Father

Faith is the confidence that what we hope for will actually happen; it gives us assurance about things we cannot see.

HEBREWS 11:1

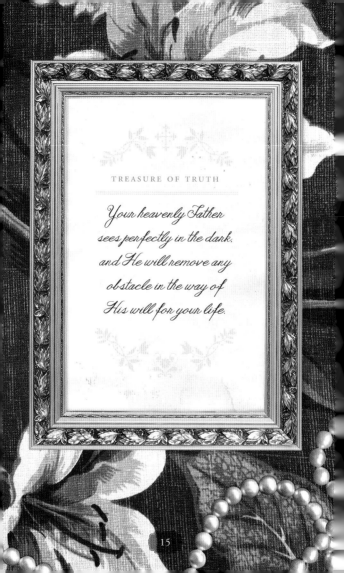

TREASURE OF TRUTH

Your heavenly Father sees perfectly in the dark, and He will remove any obstacle in the way of His will for your life.

15

You will feel lost only if you allow disappointment or desperation to direct your path.

Trust in the LORD with all your heart, and lean not on your own understanding; in all your ways acknowledge Him, and He shall direct your paths.

PROVERBS 3:5-6, NKJV

My Beloved Daughter,

When you feel desperate, you will be tempted to walk off the narrow path I designed for you. From your human perspective, this path often appears to limit your choices. However, if you choose to remain completely committed to Me, you will discover that My way leads to limitless blessings and a beautiful life. If you wander off to the wide way of desperation, you will feel lost and alone. I am always here, but I will not walk My beloved daughter down the road that leads to destruction. When you call, I will come pick you up and direct you back to My perfect will for your life. Your determination and dedication to Me will set you apart and satisfy your deepest desire to live for something beyond yourself. You are Mine; therefore, you have no need to allow disappointments or despair to direct your path any longer.

Love,
Your Father who walks with you

My Chosen Daughter,

No one can define you without your permission. I want you to be so secure in who you are in Me that nothing or no one can steal your true identity. Seek Me to find your true worth. Ask Me to guard your heart and mind from the lies of the enemy, and I will. I won't force you to call on Me, but I will never stop finding ways to display My love for you. If you could see yourself the way I do, even for a moment, no one would have the power to define who you are. Take a moment right now and think about who I am—the God who created the heavens and the earth, and the heavenly Father who calls you by name. You are My chosen one; you are set apart; you are My beloved; you are precious to Me. If there is anything other than this truth inside of you, it is not from Me. Now is the time to let go of the lie and to walk in your true identity!

Love,
Your heavenly Father forever

TREASURE OF TRUTH

How you see yourself will never change
who you are in Christ.

Once you had no identity
as a people; now you are God's
people. Once you received
no mercy; now you have
received God's mercy.

1 PETER 2:10

For God says,
"At just the right time,
I heard you. On the day
of salvation, I helped you."
Indeed, the "right time" is now.
Today is the day of salvation.

2 CORINTHIANS 6:2

TREASURE OF TRUTH

New life begins the moment your spirit becomes one
with your Savior, Jesus.

His Salvation

My Child,

I have so much I want to share with you, but you will have a heart to hear Me only when you've committed to follow My Son, Jesus, as your Savior. Your eyes can read My Word and your mind can meditate on what it means, but until your spirit is alive in Christ, you will not be transformed into the woman I created you to be. I am not asking you to surrender to My Son for My benefit but for your blessing. The life you crave is found in Christ alone. Open your heart to My one and only Son, asking Him to forgive your sins and become the Lord of your life. The moment you pray, you will be forever connected to Me and secure for now and all eternity. Just think . . . you're only one prayer away from everlasting life!

Love,
Your heavenly Father

His Freedom

My Forgiven Child,

I have walked with you all the days of your life. I've seen your past, and I know your future. I have so many plans I want to walk out with you, but as long as you're looking back, we cannot move forward together. I will stand by you, even if you choose to stand still the rest of your life. But if you will accept My gift of a new beginning, you will find the new life I have to offer. Looking at times past will only remind you of all that has gone wrong, but if you choose to let go of what's behind and fix your eyes on what's in front of you, you will be able to move forward. Trust Me when I say that there's nothing you have done or that anyone has done to you that must keep you chained to your past. I sent My Son, Jesus, to break every chain so you could be free. But only you can choose to walk out of the prison of your past and walk into the hope of a new future.

Love,
Your King who has you covered

Anyone who belongs to Christ has become a new person. The old life is gone; a new life has begun!

2 CORINTHIANS 5:17

Freedom is the prize awarded to those who leave the past behind.

23

I pray that God, the source of hope, will fill you completely with joy and peace because you trust in him. Then you will overflow with confident hope through the power of the Holy Spirit.

ROMANS 15:13

His Hope

My Precious Girl,

At times you will feel as the Israelites did before I worked through Moses to part the Red Sea. They gazed with fear into a sea of hopelessness as their Egyptian enemies headed toward them. However, as My people discovered, hopelessness is just an illusion created by the enemy. The truth is, there is no such thing as a futile situation. I am the God of hope, even when everything you love and live for appears to be drowning. When you can't swim any longer, I am your lifesaver. I am the author of your life who can rewrite and transform any tragedy into triumph. I am the one who will work all things together for your good even when it appears all has gone bad. When you don't know what to do, be still long enough to allow Me to calm the storm in your heart and part the sea that seems to lie in the way of My promises for you. If you will wait on Me, you will witness My wonders!

Love,
Your Father of miracles

TREASURE OF TRUTH

Our invisible God becomes most visible when
He is our only hope!

There is never a wrong time to get right with God and to do the right thing!

Great is his faithfulness; his mercies begin afresh each morning.

LAMENTATIONS 3:23

His Mercy

My Daughter,

I want you to know that no matter what you have
done in the past, there is never a wrong time to do
the right thing. There is no choice wrong enough,
no chain strong enough, and no time long enough
to keep you from making things right in My sight.
Now there may be those who refuse to forgive you,
but they are not the ones who will make all things
right—I am. Yes, there will be consequences to bad
choices, but I am the God who takes the wreckage
and rebuilds what is broken. Remember, you can't
change what has happened, but you can build a new
beginning . . . one choice at a time. Today is a new
day, and My mercies are new every morning. Now
pray and ask Me to show you how to make things
right, and we will work through this together, Father
and daughter.

Love,
Your Father who knows what's best

My Beloved,

Because I love you, I'm asking you to guard your heart from anyone or anything that can steal you away from Me. Remember, My love, this world offers a counterfeit life that will never fulfill you. What I create for you will satisfy your soul. What the enemy offers will satisfy your flesh for a while; however, in the end the world's way leads to destruction. If your heart wanders and you are not equipped with My Word, you will be unable to discern the difference between real faith and counterfeit religion.

As a loving Father, I ask you to invite Me to search your fragile heart and uncover what you've stored there, My girl. If you will allow me, I will shine a light into any darkness that clouds your efforts to discern good from evil. Now is the time to let Me protect you and capture your heart once again, so you don't miss the amazing ministry I can do in you and through you.

Love,
Your King who knows your heart

TREASURE OF TRUTH
Whatever has captured your heart will control you.

Guard your heart
above all else, for
it determines the course
of your life.

PROVERBS 4:23

His Perspective

My Beloved Daughter,

I know life is not fair. As I watch how the people I created treat one another, My heart breaks—just like yours does. I warned you in My Word that there will be suffering here on earth, but I have overcome this world. Don't look to people for inner strength. The power to persevere through trials cannot be found in this world. Instead, look up, and I will give you an eternal perspective and new hope. Find joy in knowing that I am coming to your rescue. When I return for you, My beloved, I will wipe away every tear, and all pain and suffering will end. For now, however, find strength in knowing that every choice you make to walk by faith and not by sight will enable you to rise above others' actions or reactions. You will find My peace by choosing to live in light of eternity from this day forward.

Love,
Your heavenly Daddy who will soon
wipe away every tear

*I have told you
all this so that you may
have peace in me.
Here on earth you will
have many trials and sorrows.
But take heart, because I have
overcome the world.*

JOHN 16:33

*Don't look at people to see God; look up to God to see
people from His perspective.*

The angel of the
LORD appeared to him
and said, "Mighty hero, the
LORD is with you!"

JUDGES 6:12

His Courage

My Daughter,

Fear is nothing more than false evidence appearing real. One of your enemy's greatest deceptions is that I am not in control. In truth, I am with you always, so you never have to fear. I am your heavenly Father, and I will prepare the way and protect you wherever I take you. Would you be willing to take a chance and trust Me, the God who loves you, to lead you through this life? If you accept My invitation to live without fear and surrender totally to Me, you will experience authentic life transformation, which only I can work inside of you. You will find the courage to step out and do something so much bigger and better than you could ever have imagined. Your soul will soar, and your faith will be energized and exercised. In the end, you will leave a legacy of faith for all who have watched you live for Me.

Love,
Your Father in heaven

TREASURE OF TRUTH

The victory belongs only to those who walk in it!

My Daughter,

I know your heart longs to see those you love reach their full potential. I am the only one, however, who has the power to change a life, and even I will not force My ways on My children. I give all people the same choice I gave you: to live for themselves, for others, or for Me. I don't want you to drain yourself trying to direct everyone else's life. Don't get discouraged when others do not listen to your good instruction; instead, pray that their hearts will be turned toward heaven so I can bring true change. Now, My beloved, come talk to Me about those you want to help. I will give you the words and good deeds, displayed through your love and life hidden in Me, that will enable you to be part of what I do in others' lives. Remember, I am the Master Gardener and you are the branch; apart from Me, nothing you do for someone else will bring permanent change.

Love,
Your Father and Life Giver

He is our God. We are the people he watches over, the flock under his care. If only you would listen to his voice today!

PSALM 95:7

34

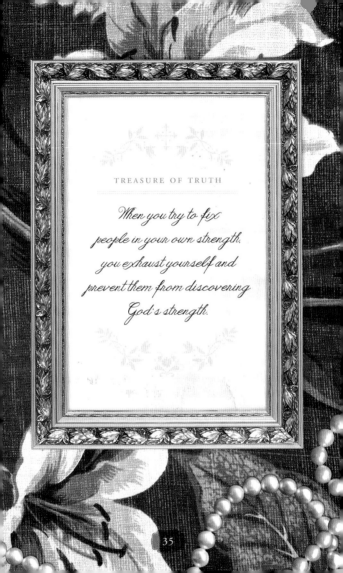

TREASURE OF TRUTH

*When you try to fix
people in your own strength,
you exhaust yourself and
prevent them from discovering
God's strength.*

35

How we choose to react will ultimately determine the outcome of our lives.

Choose my instruction rather than silver,
and knowledge rather than pure gold.

PROVERBS 8:10

His Response

My Much-Loved Daughter,

I know how hard it is to respond in a way that will glorify Me when you're hurting and feeling helpless. In such moments, you need only to call out to Me. I will calm your heart so you can control your reactions to the trials this life brings. I will never turn away from you, no matter how you act or react. Remember, too, that there is nothing you have done or said that I cannot redeem if you will come to Me and repent of your words and actions. I am your faithful Father, and it is My pleasure to turn your wrongs to right for My glory. Let Me guide you when you don't know how to react. I will give you wisdom and a way to escape from the temptation to lash out. Because you are Mine, you simply need to ask, and I will show you the way that will lead to reconciliation and revival.

Love,
Your Redeemer

His Whisper

My Treasured Daughter,

I'm never too busy to talk to you, but you must be still to hear My whisper. Turn away from the chatter that drowns out My voice, and you will begin to hear Me in your spirit. I am the voice of heaven, and I am always speaking to you in creative ways. If you look up, you will hear Me speak of the heavens' majesties; if you look at the eyes of the hurting, you will hear Me speak compassion; if you count your blessings, you will hear Me reminding you that I am always here for you. Oh, the riches I long to bestow on you today, if only you come before Me, quiet in mind and spirit!

Love,
Your Father, The voice of Heaven

> *This truth was given to me in secret,*
> *as though whispered in my ear.*
>
> JOB 4:12

*In our silence,
we will hear God
whisper wisdom and the
way forward.*

But I say, love your enemies! Pray for those who persecute you!

MATTHEW 5:44

TREASURE OF TRUTH

If you pray for your enemies, you won't become like them.

His Unconditional Love

My Precious Girl,

I know one of the hardest things I will ask you to do
is to pray for those who persecute you or your loved
ones. My request that you do so is not really for your
enemies' benefit as much as it is for yours. I know
your heart because I created you, and I know that
heartache can cause you to become someone you do
not want to be. I ask you to pray for your enemies
so you will not become like them. I ask you to pray
for your adversaries so their actions will not keep you
from acting as My beloved child. I ask you to pray
for those who do unjust things so you will learn to
let Me deal with those who cause pain to My children. If you will surrender your heart to Me instead
of to the enemy, you will find the power to overcome
and the peace that passes all understanding. I promise I will punish those who do not repent and make
things right. I am a just God, and you can trust Me.

Love,
Your protective Father in heaven

His Answer to Prayer

My Beloved Daughter,

Come to Me anytime you wish, My child. I love to hear you call out to Me for help. I long for you to witness how My mighty arm moves in response to your prayers. Don't underestimate the power of your petitions. Your words spoken on behalf of the sick will activate My Spirit to bring them comfort. Your plea for those who are hungry, either for their daily bread or the Living Bread, will lead Me to open My hand and satisfy their hunger. Your prayer for the desperate will usher in My direction. Your prayers unleash My power at work in the world. One day in heaven, you will see how your prayers affected and protected many lives, so open your heart and lips and tell your heavenly Father what is on your heart today. I will hear and respond!

Love,
Your God who loves when you pray

*And I will do whatever you ask
in my name, so that the Son may bring glory
to the Father. You may ask me for anything
in my name, and I will do it.*

JOHN 14:13-14, NIV

TREASURE OF TRUTH

*You are His daughter; therefore, you have been given
the ear of the King of kings!*

Jesus answered,
"If I want glory for
myself, it doesn't count.
But it is my Father who
will glorify me."

My Dearly Loved Daughter,

One of My greatest pleasures is giving you the desires of your heart; however, you must learn to trust that I know what you need better than you do. If you open your heart and your mind and allow Me to direct your life, you will find that what I want for you will not only fulfill you in every way, but it will also bring glory to who I am. It is only when you seek first the Kingdom of God that you will find My perfect direction. There are so many things I can and will do through you if you will empty yourself and let Me, your loving heavenly Father, fill you with every perfect and good gift. I will not force My way in, and I will love you even if you continue to live for yourself; however, I want to warn you that this world is not your final destination. What you do here and now will count for all eternity.

Love,
Your heavenly Father, who knows best

TREASURE OF TRUTH

It isn't getting what you want that satisfies; it's giving what you have for His glory.

Your past does not have to define you anymore. . . . It is finished.

I am about to do something new. See, I have already begun! Do you not see it? I will make a pathway through the wilderness. I will create rivers in the dry wasteland.

ISAIAH 43:19

46

His New Beginning

My Beloved Daughter,

You are Mine, and you are called personally by Me. That's why it is hard to watch you hold on to your past. I see you differently than you see yourself. You see what you've done, but I see what I want to do in you. You see where you've been, but I see where I want to take you. I have you covered, precious one, and I will use every mistake you've made as a tutor to make you wiser. As My daughter, you have the privilege and the choice to live an abundant life filled with joy, adventure, passion, and purpose. Don't hold on to things that hold you back from My blessings. Your past has paved the road that led you to Me. Now ask Me to do a new thing, to make a way in the wilderness, and to increase your faith in ways you never dreamed possible. Take My hand, and let's walk forward together into your new life.

Love,
Your heavenly Father

His Roadblocks

My Child,

I have asked you to lose your life so you can find your life in Me. However, many times you lose sight of why you're on earth because you get lost in trivial things. The stuff that concerns you will not matter once you are finally home. Many times I allow disappointment as a divine intervention to get you to reflect on what really matters most to you and Me. Don't allow disappointment to direct your path; instead, let it redirect you to reflect on and connect to Me again. You wouldn't question the roadblocks if you trusted Me to pave the way I want you to walk. Now, My beloved, be still and reflect on who I really am in your life. Ask yourself if you dwell in My presence or in the pursuit of happiness. In our quiet times of reflection, you will find renewed strength. I promise not a moment spent with Me will ever be wasted.

Love,
Your heavenly Daddy

TREASURE OF TRUTH

Disappointment is God's divine intervention
intended for redirection.

Now we see things imperfectly,
like puzzling reflections in a mirror,
but then we will see everything with
perfect clarity. All that I know now
is partial and incomplete, but then
I will know everything completely, just as
God now knows me completely.

1 CORINTHIANS 13:12

His Open Door

My Daughter,

Not every open door in your life is from Me. Don't immediately follow people through an open door simply because they claim to speak for Me or ask you to trust them more than Me and My Word. Don't seek counsel from those who don't walk in My wisdom or who don't live solely for Me. If I open the door, it will not cause you confusion. It will lead you to a closer relationship with Me. My open doors bring glory to My name and further My Kingdom. I am a God of order, and when I order your steps, I open doors that no man can shut. So before you walk toward a new opportunity, be sure to pray and count the cost of what you are giving up. Take an honest look at where you will be going and whether you are headed in the most effective and everlasting direction. When you seek My guidance, you will hear Me say, "This is the way, My beloved, now walk in it."

Love,
Your heavenly Father

This is
what the LORD says:
"Stop at the crossroads and
look around. Ask for the old,
godly way, and walk in it.
Travel its path, and you will
find rest for your souls."

JEREMIAH 6:16

TREASURE OF TRUTH

*Before you walk away,
count the cost of what you are leaving behind.*

There are "friends"
who destroy each other,
but a real friend sticks
closer than a brother.

PROVERBS 18:24

His Friendship

My Beloved Girl,

Everyone goes through difficult seasons in life. If this is a hard interval for someone you love, be careful not to judge him or her too harshly. Look beyond your own hurt to the pain that has caused that person to lash out or treat you unfairly. I want you to become the faithful friend you long to have when you're hurting . . . and to hang on to the good times you have shared with your loved one. Lift him or her up to Me in prayer, and I will bless this precious one in ways far beyond anything you can imagine. Once this season has passed, the bond of your relationship will be even stronger, and I will be glorified through your faithfulness!

Love,
Your Father in heaven and faithful Friend

TREASURE OF TRUTH

True friends can't be seen until conflict comes.

His Trophy

My Valued Daughter,

I know many people will define you by what you have conquered through your own abilities. Yet there is so much more to you than what's on a piece of paper or engraved on a trophy. In fact, none of your trophies will enter heaven with you. Only what has been accomplished for My Kingdom can be kept for all eternity. Think about this, My beloved: What good are the praises of people if you accomplish nothing for Me while you are walking the earth? I have already conquered death for you; now I am asking you, in My strength, to accomplish great faith works that display My majesty. These acts define the difference between a mediocre life and a miraculous life lived for Me. To become great in My Kingdom, you must live the rest of your days for an audience of one . . . Me.

Love,
The One who applauds your faith

TREASURE OF TRUTH

You are so much more than what you have accomplished.

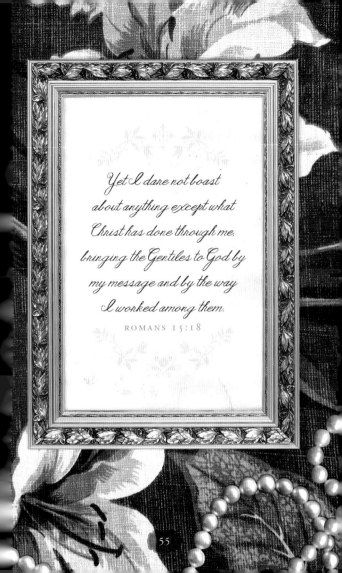

Yet I dare not boast
about anything except what
Christ has done through me,
bringing the Gentiles to God by
my message and by the way
I worked among them.

ROMANS 15:18

55

TREASURE OF TRUTH

*Don't give up
your faith because
of what you see.*

The word of the LORD holds true,
and we can trust everything he does.
He loves whatever is just and good;
the unfailing love of the LORD fills the earth.

PSALM 33:4-5

His Faithfulness

My Child,

What you see with your eyes is in physical form,
but what I am doing is in the spiritual realm. How
I long for your faith to increase so that nothing you
see will shake you or prevent you from believing in
Me. Faith is the only thing that will cause you to
keep going when everything else inside your soul
is screaming to give up. There will be crossroads in
your life when you will have to make a choice to
trust Me fully or to trust in what you see. Remember
that the trials will make you stronger and perfect
your faith so you can finish what I sent you to earth
to do. So I ask you on this day, *Whom do you choose
to trust? And do you believe I am more powerful than
your circumstance or any person who would come
against you?* The choices are yours, and they will
determine your life's direction.

Love,
Your trustworthy Father

His Heart

My Beloved Daughter,

I know loving others is risky, but what good is the love you have for Me if you will not let Me love others through you? What good is all that you have conquered and accomplished if you have not loved well? The truth, My precious girl, is that anything you accomplish minus love will equal nothing in the end. I have loved you with an unconditional, everlasting love. Nothing that you say or do changes the way I feel toward you. Now I'm asking you to love others most when they deserve it least—the same way I love you. I know what I request from you is not easy, but if you will draw on My strength, you will find that perfect love casts out fear. Even if those you love let you down, I will reward you for all eternity because you chose to love them in a way that brought glory to Me.

Love,
Your Father who has a never-ending love for you

TREASURE OF TRUTH

What good is love if you don't give it away?

*If I gave everything
I have to the poor and even
sacrificed my body, I could boast
about it; but if I didn't love others,
I would have gained nothing.*

1 CORINTHIANS 13:3

*There is a way
that seems right to a man,
but in the end it leads
to death.*

PROVERBS 16:25, NIV

TREASURE OF TRUTH

Just because it works does not make it right.

My Daughter,

You can always find ways to get what you want or to get your way. Just because something works, though, does not mean it's right in My sight. What good could come from using someone or something to manipulate others, or even to try to move people with your own good intentions? Without Me and My righteousness, anything that seems to be working ultimately will not last. I know that many times doing the right thing in My sight seems useless. Remember, though, that there is something more important than results, and that is My righteousness in you. What you do My way will ultimately build a foundation of integrity, which will be rewarded with My favor and blessing on your life. It is what you do when no one but Me sees that truly reflects your heart and commitment to Me. Now together, let's make right whatever is wrong.

Love,
Your King who knows what works

His Harmony

My Precious Child,

Living in harmony is like delighting in a sweet song that calms your very soul. Yet I know such unity is difficult to orchestrate. That is why I want you to learn to appreciate the different ways I have wired every person in your life. They are not you and you are not them. You each have been given distinctive gifts to enrich one another's perspective. I know you always take a risk when you invest your heart in other people, but remember no one will love you as perfectly as I do. Come to Me to satisfy your wants and needs, and you will be able to meet the needs of those you love. Look for ways to bring unity, and encourage those in your life to seek My assurance even more than they seek yours. With Me at the center of life, you will find the harmony all human hearts long for in their relationships.

Love,
Your heavenly Father

*May God, who gives this patience
and encouragement, help you live in
complete harmony with each other, as is
fitting for followers of Christ Jesus. Then
all of you can join together with one
voice, giving praise and glory to God,
the Father of our Lord Jesus Christ.*

ROMANS 15:5-6

TREASURE OF TRUTH

If we are not unified, God is not glorified.

Pride goes before destruction, and haughtiness before a fall.

PROVERBS 16:18

His Direction

My Daughter,

Many times your ways may appear to be better than Mine, at least in your own mind. What I ask may at times feel uncomfortable or sacrificial, but I would rather you be in discomfort than experience the destruction of living your own way. I'm asking you to trust Me, even when it's hard to do what I ask of you in My Word. When you obey, honor, and respect Me as your heavenly Father, I will give you so much more than what you willingly give up for Me. In the end, you will stay strong in your faith, and your heart will remain at peace regardless of any trials this life brings. My ways are not your ways, My beloved. They are higher and they are greater. My rules are effective, but they are not easy. It is in your righteous discomfort that you will remain safe and secure under My wing.

Love,
Your God of comfort

TREASURE OF TRUTH
Discomfort is far better than destruction.

TREASURE OF TRUTH

Your Father sees perfectly what you cannot. He will remove any obstacle in the way of His will.

For God, who said,
"Let there be light in the darkness,"
has made this light shine in our hearts
so we could know the glory of God that
is seen in the face of Jesus Christ.

2 CORINTHIANS 4:6

66

His Light

My Beloved Daughter,

There will be times when I seem to be allowing you to walk in the darkness. You never have to worry when it is dark because I am your light. As your faithful Father, I don't want you to wander away from Me. If it takes darkness to make you desperate for My light, then it will be worth losing your sight so you can see Me clearly. When you feel lost, don't look to others for the light; get on your knees and call out to Me. I will come to your rescue every time. Your faith will soar when you let go of what you see in the natural light. As long as you let My Word and My instruction illuminate where you walk, you will not stumble or fear what you cannot see. My desire for you, My daughter, is that you no longer be controlled by what you see but live by what you know to be true about Me. From this day forward, may you choose to never again doubt in the darkness what you know to be true in the light!

Love,
Your faithful Father

His Masterpiece

My Treasure,

I know you don't see it, but you are My masterpiece.
I have been carving your character through trials,
and I am displaying My grace through your weaknesses. But now I am asking you to open your eyes
and say yes to all the work I want to do through you.
I am ready to appoint you as an ambassador of hope
to the hurting and an agent of comfort to those who
feel worthless inside.

I long to display My glory and marvelous plan
for your life for all to see, but I love you too much
to give you more than your heart can handle. So I
encourage you to pray and ask Me to help you get
your heart ready to watch the wonderful work I will
do in you and through you, starting today if you
are willing.

Love,
Your God of creation

For we are God's masterpiece.
He has created us anew in Christ Jesus, so we can do
the good things he planned for us long ago.

EPHESIANS 2:10

TREASURE OF TRUTH

Our Potter does His greatest work when the clay is soft and ready to be molded into something beautiful.

His Holy Spirit

My Princess Warrior,

Your inward battles don't mean you are weak.
Do you not know by now that My Holy Spirit is
stronger than any struggle you have? I will give you
victory because He lives in you. I don't want you to
beat yourself up any longer for your inward battles.
Instead, learn to surrender to My voice of conviction
and correction. Then free yourself by confessing any
sin to Me. When you're weak, call to Me and let Me
be your strength. I am the only one who can carry
you when you feel like you cannot carry on. I am
here to help you become the woman who you long
to be and whom I created you to be. We will work
through this together, and I will never give up on
you, no matter how long it takes you to get right
with Me.

Love,
Your faithful Father

Keep watch and pray,
so that you will not
give in to temptation.
For the spirit is willing,
but the body is weak!

MATTHEW 26:41

TREASURE OF TRUTH

Inward battles don't mean that you are weak . . . but that
you are a warrior fighting to do what is right.

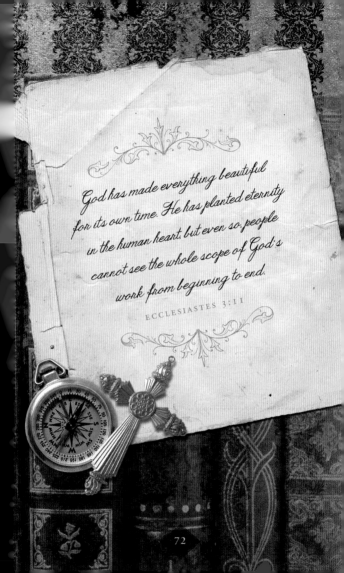

God has made everything beautiful for its own time. He has planted eternity in the human heart, but even so, people cannot see the whole scope of God's work from beginning to end.

ECCLESIASTES 3:11

His Timing

My Beloved Daughter,

My plan for your life does not have an expiration date, but it does unfold in My perfect timing. If you move ahead of Me, you will feel lost. If you stay behind, you will feel left out. But if you stay close to Me, you will move to the timing of My heartbeat. I know the plans I have for you, and they will come to pass. Right now, I have appointed you to love whoever is in front of you and to meet the needs of those I have entrusted to your care. As you begin to be faithful with the little things, I will begin to give you the bigger things I planned for you all along. Now, My beloved, is the time to ask Me to use you in someone's life today.

Love,
Your Father whose timing is perfect

TREASURE OF TRUTH

God's timing is just as important as His will itself.

My Blessed Daughter,

Oh, how I'm pleased when you obey Me because I love to reward you with everlasting blessings! When you feel trapped and need to break free from the strongholds of this world, let Me search your heart and see what holds you back from My blessings. If you will be still long enough for Me to shine My light in the dark areas, I will help you find your way out of any sin that entangles you. What I ask for you is not just for My glory; it is for your good. No temporary pleasure can satisfy your soul the way I can. Not only that, even your children's children will be blessed if you love Me with all your heart and obey Me all the days of your life. Now is the time to get your heart right so you can live in the freedom I offer you!

Love,
Your everlasting Father

> *You will experience all these blessings if you*
> *obey the LORD your God.*
>
> DEUTERONOMY 28:2

The Lord's love is unconditional; many of His promises are not!

TREASURE OF TRUTH

When you have

no idea what to do . . .

be still and wait on God.

Be still, and know that I am God!

PSALM 46:10

76

My Beloved Girl,

When you're in trouble, you may have no idea what to do. In such times, I need you to do nothing but be still and let me fight whatever battle you are facing. I know it's difficult for you to remain at rest when you want to act or when you feel anxious. However, if you react based on what you feel, you will lose. When you can't calm down, call to Me and I will soothe your fearful heart. You may not see the storm on the outside coming to an end, but the storm inside your soul will end in My presence. I can give you the peace that passes all understanding as I work on your behalf. Simply wait in a quiet place under My wing. Hear Me whisper even now: "Be still and know that I am the God who has taken control of what you cannot."

Love,
Your King

His Attention

My Precious Girl,

I see your hard work and dedication to others. I know that often the wonderful ways you help others go unnoticed and unappreciated. But that does not make them useless, My love. What you do and the way you serve bring Me great pleasure, and what I see in secret, I will reward openly in heaven. Don't get discouraged. Find joy in knowing that I am pleased with you. Remember that even My Son, Jesus, did not come to be served but to serve others. It wasn't until His earthly life was over that people really understood all that I sent Him to do for them. Today, you are a representative of heaven on earth, and all that you do enthusiastically for My glory will never be wasted. Now smile, knowing that your loving Father is also your faithful rewarder of every good work.

Love,
Your God who watches over you

TREASURE OF TRUTH
He is the God who sees you when no one else does.

Be strong and immovable.
Always work enthusiastically
for the Lord, for you know
that nothing you do for the
Lord is ever useless.

1 CORINTHIANS 15:58

Then the man said,
"Let me go, for the dawn is breaking!"
But Jacob said,
"I will not let you go unless
you bless me."

GENESIS 32:26

TREASURE OF TRUTH

Don't forfeit all God has for you;
do whatever it takes to fight for it instead!

My Daughter,

I have much to give you, but you will have to fight for much of it. There is an enemy who wants to steal every good thing I offer you, and there is also an enemy inside of you—your internal voice that whispers that you don't deserve the goodness I want to pour into you. Many times you forfeit the blessings rather than fight for them. I want you to be willing, instead, to do whatever it takes to get all I have for you. Take a moment and reflect on who you are in Me. You are a warrior anointed to fight for the things worth fighting for. Do not give in to the temptation to walk off the battlefield. Instead, I ask you to wrestle with your insecurities and inadequacies. As you do, you will find that I am worth every ounce of energy and effort you invest in fighting to further My Kingdom on earth.

Love,
Your King who is ready to bless you

His Perfect Gifts

My Blessed One,

I have gifted you with a special talent, something only you can do and something only you can use. You may not see what it is or value what it's worth, but I have created you to use it for the purpose of carving a mark of faith on the hearts of those you love. You can decide to bury this talent. If you do, no one will ever see it and you will miss the purpose of your life. Or you can use the talent to bring attention to yourself, and no lives will ever be changed by what you do. Instead, I ask you to dedicate to Me all that you are and all that you are equipped to do so I can multiply every good and perfect gift I have placed inside of you. The talent I have given you is of value only if it is spent on others for My glory, not yours.

Love,
Your God, the Gift Giver

So I was afraid and went out and hid your talent in the ground. See, here is what belongs to you.

MATTHEW 25:25, NIV

TREASURE OF TRUTH

Your talent is too valuable to waste.

83

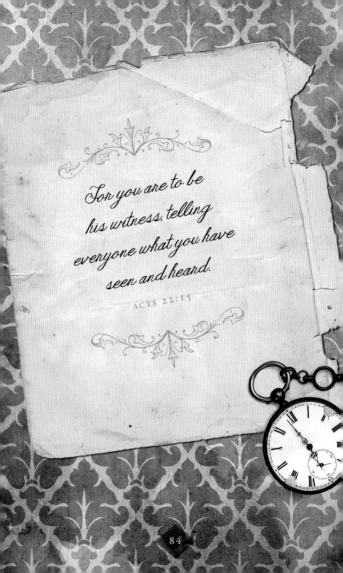

For you are to be
his witness, telling
everyone what you have
seen and heard.

ACTS 22:15

His Witness

My Precious Daughter,

I want you to think back to the time when you did not know Me personally. Do you remember how lost you felt? Or how meaningless life seemed to be? Even now, many people feel alone because they do not know who I am or what I have done for them. I have a request: I would like you to go and tell others of your love for Me. I know it may feel uncomfortable, but I have called you to be My witness. Whatever I ask of you, I will equip you to do. I will go before you to prepare hearts to hear you. I won't force you to represent Me, and I will love you no matter what you decide, but I'm asking you to search your heart and ask yourself, *Why am I here?* and *What am I really living for?* If you live for Me, step into your appointed position as My messenger of hope to a world that is hurting and needs to hear of My love.

Love,
Your King who reached out to you

TREASURE OF TRUTH

Our lives may be the only Bible some people will ever read.

Don't give up what you want most for a moment of pleasure.

I said to myself,
"Come on, let's try pleasure. Let's look for the
'good things' in life." But I found that this, too,
was meaningless.

ECCLESIASTES 2:1

86

His Pleasure

My Precious Girl,

This world will offer many things that will give you a moment of pleasure and a lifetime of pain. The enemy of your soul rules this earth for a while, but greater is My Spirit in you than he who rules the world. Stay close to Me and be equipped with My Word because the enemy will tempt you and try to make you believe that I am not enough for you. He will offer a counterfeit to everything I have created in an attempt to steal your heart. I created love, and he offers lust. I created a way for you to have a real relationship with Me through My Son, Jesus, and he offers an artificial religion that leaves My children feeling far from Me. I created truth, and he is the father of lies. I am your defender, and he is your accuser. I am your protector, and he is your persecutor. If you seek after Me to find purpose and pleasure, you will not only be more than satisfied, you will be safe and secure under My wing.

Love,
Your King

His Favor

My Daughter,

Many times in your life you will make something
happen on your own that appears good. You may
even convince yourself that it indicates My approval
and is My gift to you. I want you to remember this,
My beloved daughter: If what you're receiving does
not point to Me, then it is not from Me. Whatever I give will draw you closer to Me or be used
to further My Kingdom on earth. I tell you this so
you will always hear My voice clearly and be able
to discern what is My gift and what is not. I created
you for so much more than flavorless life; I want you
to taste what it's like to live a fruitful life, walking in
My favor every day.

Love,
Your good and gracious King

If it is true that you look favorably on me,
let me know your ways so I may understand you more
fully and continue to enjoy your favor. And remember
that this nation is your very own people.

EXODUS 33:13

TREASURE OF TRUTH

If no spiritual fruit comes from that pleasure . . . it isn't an offshoot of God's favor.

His Written Word

My Beloved,

I never want you to take My Word for granted.
I have written it so you will know who you are,
who I am, how to live, why you are here, and where
you are going. My Word will give you wisdom; My
Word will become the sword that protects you from
the attacks of the enemy. My Word is a lamp to your
feet and a light to your path. My Word is powerful; My Word is promise; My Word will live on
long after you're gone. My Word will increase your
faith and strengthen you when you are weak. My
Word has always been and will always be. As your
heavenly Father, I'm asking you to make My Word
the very thing that feeds your spirit, your mind, and
your soul. If you will make time for My Word, I will
reveal Myself to you in the most wonderful ways
you can imagine. Now, My love, open your Bible
and let Me speak to you.

Love,
Your God, the Author of the written Word

Heaven and earth will pass away, but my words will never pass away.

LUKE 21:33, NIV

TREASURE OF TRUTH

The Word of God is the only word that really matters.

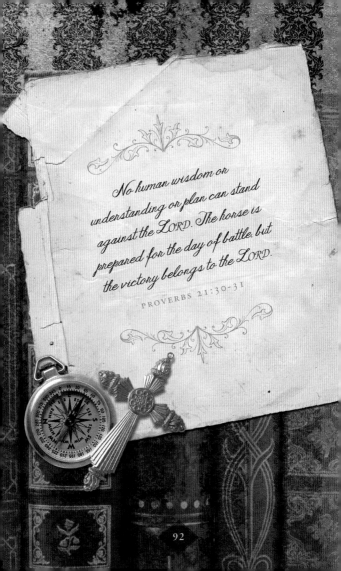

No human wisdom or
understanding or plan can stand
against the LORD. The horse is
prepared for the day of battle, but
the victory belongs to the LORD.

PROVERBS 21:30-31

His Preparation

My Child,

I call you by name. You are Mine, and you are being prepared for great and mighty things. I know sometimes life does not seem fair, and you may even believe I have forsaken you. The truth, My love, is that the painful places you have walked have prepared your heart to receive even more of Me. The times you came to a crossroads in your life and were tempted to walk away from Me were tests of faith designed to prepare you for where I want to take you now. Because I love you, I will remove anything and anyone who gets in the way of the wonderful works I want to do through you. You are not called to be comfortable; you are called to be fruitful. I am your loving Father and the Gardener of your life; therefore, My pruning will prepare you for a beautiful life that will be remembered by all who watched you live surrendered to Me.

Love,
Your Father who loves you

TREASURE OF TRUTH

The blessing and benefits from My preparation
will soon be seen.

His Loved Ones

My Daughter,

I know it's sometimes hard for you to place your loved ones in My hands. But it is in the moments that you choose to trust Me with those you love that I will become most real and visible to you. I know how much you long to be loved by them. I see that you want the best for them and are willing to sacrifice anything for them. However, you cannot give them what I can, so I ask you to point them to Me so you can be free from being controlled by your love for others. They ultimately are Mine, and I am the only one who can give them the love they will need to love you. If you will rest in My faithfulness and trust that I am a Father who knows best, then your loved ones will no longer rule your heart—I will. Remember, I give "perfect love," which casts out fear. So lay down your fear and trust Me from this day forward with those you hold closest to your heart.

Love,
Your Father who loves you and those you love

Acknowledge that the LORD is God! He made us,
and we are his. We are his people, the sheep of his pasture.

PSALM 100:3

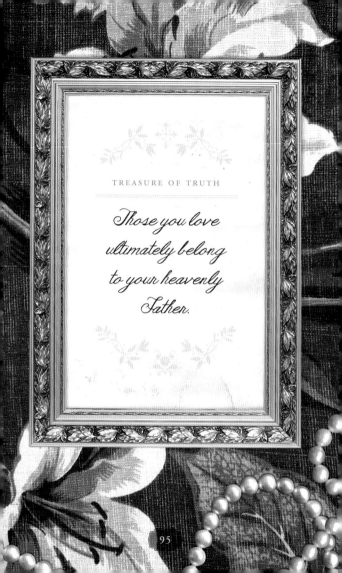

TREASURE OF TRUTH

*Those you love
ultimately belong
to your heavenly
Father.*

*Our legacy
of faith means so much more
than the life we wanted.*

He is the faithful God who keeps his covenant
for a thousand generations and lavishes his unfailing
love on those who love him and obey his commands.

DEUTERONOMY 7:9

96

His Legacy

My Beloved Daughter,

Your life is not just about you; your legacy of faith will live on long after you're gone. Every time you choose to lay down what you want so you can follow My will, you make a deposit in the next generation. Every hard choice you make for Me, every act of courageous faith, will birth a blessing for you and all those you hold dear. Every selfless deed you do to bring glory to My name will point another person to Me. Every test of faith that you pass will be greatly rewarded. Never underestimate the power of My promise. Your love and obedience to Me will enable you to leave the greatest inheritance you could possibly give to your children and grandchildren. That's because I am a faithful God who blesses a thousand generations of those who love and obey Me all the days of their lives. . . . This promise is yours!

Love,
Your heavenly Father who keeps His promise

His Transforming Love

My Daughter,

You are not of this world anymore because you belong to Me. As My daughter, you represent heaven on earth by the way you live. If you will let Me, I will transform you into the beautiful creation I called you to be. After all, I am the one who created you, and I know everything about you. I adore you, and I want to do more for you. Let Me start by revealing who I am, the King of kings and Lord of lords. If you will come to Me each morning, I will share something new with you that will transform the way you see yourself. I don't want you to settle for less than I have for you. It's time to let yourself live for a greater cause—Me and My Kingdom—so that you, transformed by My love, can shine on earth as a reflection of Me.

Love,
Your transforming King

TREASURE OF TRUTH

Amazing change begins in us as we choose
to live for our King.

*Don't copy the behavior
and customs of this world,
but let God transform you into a
new person by changing the way you
think. Then you will learn to know
God's will for you, which is good
and pleasing and perfect.*

ROMANS 12:2

Every day of my life
was recorded in your book.
Every moment was laid out
before a single day
had passed.

PSALM 139:16

TREASURE OF TRUTH

*If God is not writing your life story,
the pages will have no ultimate meaning.*

My Beloved Daughter,

I am the Author of your life story. I want to fill the pages with many amazing faith adventures, but first you must surrender the pen to Me. You can spend your days trying to write in your own wisdom and creativity, but I fear you will end up with a meaningless story that wasn't written with eternity in view. Don't despair if you insisted on writing the opening chapters yourself: it's not too late to turn your story over to Me. No matter where you are now, I can determine where you'll end up if you allow Me to redefine your character and fill the rest of the pages with My story lived out through you. When this life is over, you will look back and see how I made all circumstances work together for your good. Your story will then be remembered for all eternity, and each page will be colored with My words and My will.

Love,
Your Father

His Solace

My Daughter,

I know it's hard for you when you suffer or see others suffering. But pain is a part of this life, My beloved. Many times following Me will cost you your comfort. Even My Son, Jesus, asked Me for another way out of His anguish; yet it was only through His suffering that your heart could be connected to Mine. I will be with you through anything you must endure for My sake. I was with Daniel in the lions' den and with Joseph when he was falsely accused and thrown in prison. I warn you in My Word that there will be troubles in life, but I have overcome the world. If you are suffering for My name's sake, you will be greatly rewarded when I return and all suffering comes to an end forever. For now, hold on to hope and watch Me use your suffering in supernatural ways.

Love,
Your Father who feels your pain

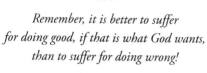

Remember, it is better to suffer
for doing good, if that is what God wants,
than to suffer for doing wrong!

I PETER 3:17

TREASURE OF TRUTH

What good is our way if we are not doing God's good will?

Today I have given you the choice between life and death, between blessings and curses. Now I call on heaven and earth to witness the choice you make. Oh, that you would choose life, so that you and your descendants might live!

DEUTERONOMY 30:19

My Beloved Daughter,

Every day you must choose between walking with
Me or walking far from Me. You decide whether
to live under My shield of protection or to push
it away by your own disobedience. Though you
must decide whether to follow Me, My beloved,
I will never stop pursuing you or showing you the
benefits of living completely surrendered to My
ways. I love you with an everlasting love, and it
is always My first choice to bless you. If you will
choose Me, I will give you everything you need to
stay faithful and true to your convictions. You will
see My mighty hand move on your behalf in all
circumstances when you give your full attention
to My Word. Remember this: anything I ask of
you is for your best interest and everlasting blessing.
My heart's desire is that you would choose life.

Love,
Your Lord who chose you

TREASURE OF TRUTH

*A timely life choice can change the course of the rest
of your life.*

TREASURE OF TRUTH

What you willingly give up determines how much God can give to you.

"Bring the whole tithe into the storehouse,
that there may be food in my house. Test me in this,"
says the LORD Almighty, "and see if I will not throw open
the floodgates of heaven and pour out so much blessing
that there will not be room enough to store it."

MALACHI 3:10, NIV

His Tithe

My Daughter,

Share what you have for the furthering of My Kingdom, and then watch Me pour out a blessing too
big for you to contain. It is impossible for you to
outgive your heavenly Father. The more you give for
My Kingdom, the more I will give to you. I'm asking
you to test Me by giving Me a part of everything
I originally gave to you. Whatever you hold on to
tighter than you hold on to Me will have a hold on
you. I want to pour out My provision on you, but
I won't give to you what I can't give away through
you. I want to free you from the love of money and
possessions. Open your heart and give, as I lead you
to a rich life that money cannot buy.

Love,
Your Father who loves to give

His Touch

My Precious Daughter,

I want you to know that I am only one whisper away. In those times when you need a special touch from Me, I will come and be your comfort and your healer. Because you are My beloved, you have access to Me anytime. I am never too busy to reach out to you. I love to hear you call My name when you're in need. Don't let your discomfort deceive you into believing I am not here. Believe that I am the one who can take care of you and who carries your burdens and feels your pain. I am compassionate and cannot resist you when you cry out to Me. When all hope of healing is gone, you will know Me as the true healer of your heart and soul.

Love,
Your heavenly Daddy

She thought,
"If I can just touch his robe, I will be healed."

MATTHEW 9:21

TREASURE OF TRUTH

*One touch
from the Savior
is all it takes to be
made whole.*

His Refining Fire

My Daughter,

When you are in a fire and see no way out, know that I am there with you and will never let the flames consume you. You may wonder why I do not rescue you from the fire right away. While I will always come to your aid eventually, it isn't the rescue that prepares you for the call I have on your life. It is the perseverance you develop in the heat of a battle that readies you for your divine purpose. I will never allow you to be in a blaze that burns you up or burns you out. Instead, I will use it to purify you for a greater purpose and to prepare you for the amazing plans I have for you. Rest assured, I am in the fire with you, and I will never leave you alone to fight the fire by yourself. Once the flames die out, you will emerge beautifully purified. Your faith will burn brightly so that the world will see that you are Mine.

Love,
Your purifying Father

"Look!"
Nebuchadnezzar shouted.
"I see four men, unbound,
walking around in the fire
unharmed! And the fourth
looks like a god!"

DANIEL 3:25

 TREASURE OF TRUTH

You won't know true faith until you are thrown
into the fire.

111

Fix your thoughts on what is true,
and honorable, and right, and pure,
and lovely, and admirable.
Think about things that are excellent
and worthy of praise.

PHILIPPIANS 4:8

His Thoughts

My Daughter,

My desire is that your heart and mind would be in perfect peace and free from the worries and negativity of this world. This supernatural peace is yours by the power of My Holy Spirit and through your choice to meditate on what is true, honorable, right, pure, and lovely. Choose to wake up each day and put Me in the forefront of your mind. Discipline your mind to think about what is worthy of praise. Guard your thoughts, My beloved, because they will become your actions, and your actions will become your destiny. If you cannot find anything in front of you that is worthy of praise, look up and praise Me for who I am. Allow My promises to fill your heart with joy. Keep your mind fixed on eternity. Without My perspective, there may be much that you are missing. Allow Me to open your eyes so your thoughts are controlled by faith, not by sight.

Love,
Your King who is always thinking of you

TREASURE OF TRUTH

Whatever you fix your mind on will control you.

His Illumination

My Chosen One,

Don't be afraid of the darkness because I have called you to be the light. And the darker the times get, the more you will have the opportunity to display My glorious light. I have anointed you to be like a star that points to heaven and a light that leads others to My throne. This honor is not something you earned, My beloved. It is a gift I want to unwrap inside of you so you can give My love away every day. The more time you spend in My presence, the more your life in Me will become a light that shines joy, love, and peace on those who are lost. Now let Me illuminate every area of your heart with My loving-kindness and mercy so you can walk the rest of your days living like the star I know you are!

Love,
The Light of the World

For once you were full of darkness,
but now you have light from the Lord.
So live as people of light!

EPHESIANS 5:8

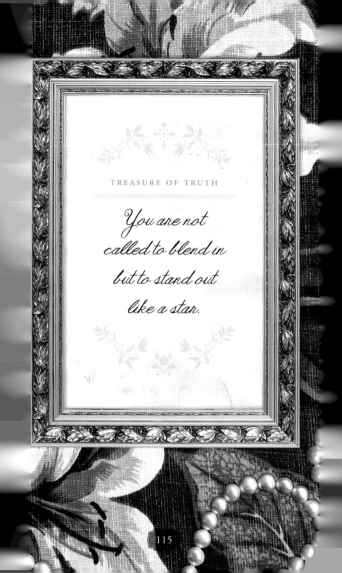

TREASURE OF TRUTH

You are not called to blend in but to stand out like a star.

TREASURE OF TRUTH

Don't doubt in the darkness
what you know to be true
in His light.

Jesus told him,
"I am the way, the truth, and the life.
No one can come to the Father except through me."

JOHN 14:6

His Truth

My Daughter,

The enemy of your soul wants to steal the truth and feed you lies, just as he did to My first daughter, Eve, in the Garden of Eden. My deepest desire is that you walk in the truth and let go of every lie. In fact, you never have to walk in lies again, My beloved. Instead, seek the truth that is found in My Word. Hide that Word in your heart. My truth will set you free. It will enable you to discern right from wrong. It will keep you on the straight and narrow road. It will remind you that you are on the pathway to your eternal home. Hold on to Scripture, the lifesaver that will keep you from drowning in deception.

Love,
Your one and only Way to true life

His Reward

My Daughter,

Many times you grow weary and wonder if what you are doing matters or makes a difference. I want to assure you that anything you do to please Me will never be useless. Even if you never receive a single reward here on earth, I see your heart and your dedication to doing My work. One day I will return, and everyone will see the eternally significant things you did for Me. My reward is so much better than the praise of man or money. When you invest your time and talent to further My Kingdom, you need never look back on your life with regret. Instead, you can look ahead to great rewards. Keep doing your work as unto Me, and I will keep storing up your everlasting treasures in heaven.

Love,
Your Father and reward

TREASURE OF TRUTH

*Riches in heaven cannot be bought, but they can
be earned right now!*

"Look, I am coming soon,
bringing my reward with me
to repay all people
according to their deeds."

REVELATION 22:12

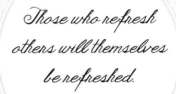

Those who refresh others will themselves be refreshed.

PROVERBS 11:25

TREASURE OF TRUTH

When you refresh others with God, the Living Water,
you will find refreshment for your own soul.

His Refreshment

My Redeemed One,

There will be times when you feel your faith is drying up and your soul is dehydrated. When life's trials and busyness have left you parched or stagnant, remember that I am here, waiting for you to come to Me to be revived. Let your soul thirst for Me alone. I am the Living Water; no one knows how to refresh your soul and water you with My Word like I do. I see your needs before you do, and I am here to pour My grace into you so you can pour out My love to others. The beauty is that you will then be energized by your efforts to bring My living water to other thirsty people.

Love,
The Lord who refreshes

My Daughter,

I sent you My Holy Spirit to teach you how much you need a Savior and how you should walk in faith as My chosen child. Your faith will be most valuable to you when you are being tested. Life is full of such trials; in fact, almost every day something will test your faith and cause you to question what you're made of. Even in those moments when you feel you have failed, I have much to teach you. Failure is never final with Me. Every time you allow a test to make you stronger and draw you closer to Me, I will redeem your disappointments. Now ask Me for wisdom and let your mistakes become your tutors. Let My Word be the tool you use to study the art of life.

Love,
Your heavenly Teacher

*Every test of faith gives you more
knowledge of God's grace.*

Examine yourselves to see if your faith is genuine.
Test yourselves. Surely you know that Jesus Christ is among
you; if not, you have failed the test of genuine faith.

2 CORINTHIANS 13:5

You were running
the race so well.
Who has held you back
from following the truth?

GALATIANS 5:7

His Race

My Daughter,

There is no greater race than the one I have prepared
for you. You are called to run until the day you cross
the finish line of this life. You will sometimes feel
exhilarated as you run your course; at other times,
you will feel weary and worn-out from the heaviness
as this world slows you down. Some people will
applaud your efforts, but others will discourage you
or try to hold you back from giving your best for
Me. If you run for the praise of people, you will lose
sight of your goal and ultimately lose your reward
in heaven. That's why it's critical that you keep your
eyes fixed on Me alone. I am your eternal life coach,
and you are running to win souls for My Kingdom.
Don't waste your days running on empty. Let Me
nourish your body, mind, and spirit so you can be
prepared to win!

Love,
Your loving Coach

TREASURE OF TRUTH

What good is running for the praises of people if you
accomplish nothing for the Kingdom of God?

TREASURE OF TRUTH

With God, the giant is not too big to hit—it is too big to miss!

If God is for us, who can ever be against us?

ROMANS 8:31

126

His Might

My Child,

I am your strong and mighty Father, and you have nothing to fear when I am on your side. Your perspective, however, is a choice, My love. You can feed your fear with your words or you can fuel your faith by standing on My Word. You can focus on the size of the giants in your life, or you can focus on how big I am. My history of faithfulness and victories on the battlefield should be enough to give you confidence in Me. I am the God who gave Moses the miraculous ability to lead My people out of slavery and to the Promised Land. I was with David when he faced a giant, and I was with Daniel in the lions' den. In fact, I am with every one of My children who faces enemies. If you try standing up to giants on your own, you might start out with boldness, but eventually you will be crippled by fear. Instead, walk in My confidence. When you do, you will become unstoppable and immovable.

Love,
Your Father and powerful Protector

His Rest

My Daughter,

I have set you apart to do much for My Kingdom. Wherever I guide you, I will provide you with everything you need to accomplish My mission—including refreshment. I know what you need because I made every part of you, so be sure to honor and surrender to My command to rest. Don't forget that even I, the God who created the heavens and the earth, took a day to rest from all My work. If you keep the Sabbath day, you will be able to conquer so much more because you are doing your work My way. As your loving heavenly Father, I ask you to take Me at My Word and trust Me enough with all you have to do . . . that you can take a break from it. If you do, I will bless all your work for Me.

Love,
Your God of rest

For all who have entered into God's rest have rested from their labors, just as God did after creating the world.

HEBREWS 4:10

TREASURE OF TRUTH

If the devil can't make you bad, his next trick will be to try to burn you out.

His Warfare

My Daughter,

Spiritual warfare is not a game. You, My child, are in a very real battle with darkness every day. The enemy of your soul prowls around like a raging lion, waiting for an opportunity to devour you. His greatest weapon is temptation; his strategy is to tantalize you with anything that will weaken your desire for Me. Don't be afraid to run to Me when you feel tempted. I know everything about you already, and I will always provide you with a way of escape. The enemy cannot or will not win as long as you stay close to Me, under My covering. Grab hold of the promises of protection and peace that are hidden in My Word, and remember that you can stand up against anything that threatens you when you're on your knees in prayer. I, your heavenly Father, will fight for you; don't drain your strength trying to wage spiritual battles with human understanding.

Love,
Your King, the great escape

Stay alert!
Watch out for your
great enemy, the devil.
He prowls around like a roaring
lion, looking for someone to
devour. Stand firm against him,
and be strong in your faith.

1 PETER 5:8-9

TREASURE OF TRUTH

The best posture to engage in spiritual warfare is standing
strong after spending time on your knees in prayer.

You can make
many plans, but the LORD's
purpose will prevail.

PROVERBS 19:21

MY TREASURE
His Agenda

My Beloved Daughter,

Many times you pray and ask Me to bless your
plans. If you ever wonder why I don't seem to
answer your pleas that your own strategies succeed,
remember that I have a plan for your life that fits
into My Kingdom agenda. I love when you come
to Me with your requests, but I love it even more
when you submit to Me and ask Me which way you
should go. I want you to spend your time wisely
by following a plan that is effective and everlasting.
You may not always understand why some of the
good-sounding plans that you have made do not
succeed, but one day you will see how I worked
everything together for your good and for My glory.
For now, I ask you to seek My agenda and let My
plans prevail in your life.

Love,
Your Master Planner

TREASURE OF TRUTH

God's detours are His divine interventions.

My Daughter,

I know life is not fair. In My Word, I warn you that your faith will undergo trials and testing. Don't look at what you see; hang on to what you know to be true about Me. If you ask for it, I will give you spiritual sight so you can see your way through the dark days of life. If pain has burrowed its way inside your soul, unlock the prison door that holds your heart hostage and invite Me in. I know it may be hard, but it will be far harder to stay locked up and alone. I will lovingly wait outside the door until you are ready to have Me escort you out onto the path that leads to abundant life and freedom. When My Spirit abides in you, He will help you see beyond the pain and find the passion to comfort others in need. It's time to be free!

Love,
Your Father, who makes everything right

TREASURE OF TRUTH

Many times pain prepares you for a purpose.

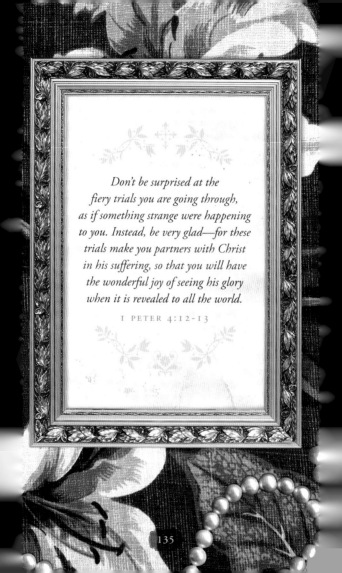

*Don't be surprised at the
fiery trials you are going through,
as if something strange were happening
to you. Instead, be very glad—for these
trials make you partners with Christ
in his suffering, so that you will have
the wonderful joy of seeing his glory
when it is revealed to all the world.*

1 PETER 4:12-13

135

You can't stop time, but you can choose to embrace every hour.

For everything there is a season,
a time for every activity under heaven.

ECCLESIASTES 3:1

His Seasons

My Precious Girl,

There will be sweet seasons in your life that you won't want to end, along with seasons that seem hard and long. There will be times to laugh, but there will also be times to cry. There will be times when you plant seeds in people's lives, and there will be times to let loved ones go so they can grow. You will have friends whom I place in your life for a season and others who will be there throughout your life. When I want you to mature, you may find yourself in a season of pruning that will make you even more fruitful. The key to contentment, My love, is to seek Me in every season and to look for what I want you to learn about life during that time. I want you to embrace all the seasons throughout your life, knowing that I created every one of them. Through each one, hold on to the hope you have in Me. Then you will truly be able to embrace life as it comes.

Love,
Your Father, who cultivates you through every season

His Bride

My Precious One,

You are invited to join Me for the biggest wedding feast in history. On that glorious day, I will come to rescue you from this world. We will celebrate the ways you lived your life well for Me. I know it is impossible for you to imagine now, but this dream will become reality. On that day, I will wipe away every tear. There will be no more sickness or death; the old order of this world will be gone. The day of this feast will mark the first day of the rest of your eternal life. Now take a moment and dream of that day. When you do, whatever is concerning you will lose its grip on your soul, and you will soar above your circumstances. You will know that this, too, shall pass—but My love for you never will.

Love,
Your Lord who is coming soon

TREASURE OF TRUTH

Happily ever after is reality for those who love the Lord.

The Spirit and the bride say, "Come."
Let anyone who hears this say, "Come."
Let anyone who is thirsty come.
Let anyone who desires drink freely
from the water of life.

REVELATION 22:17

*And I am convinced that nothing
can ever separate us from God's
love. Neither death nor life, neither
angels nor demons, neither our fears
for today nor our worries about
tomorrow—not even the powers of
hell can separate us from God's love.*

ROMANS 8:38

TREASURE OF TRUTH

Nothing can ever separate you from your Father's love.

His Commitment

My Daughter,

My love for you is unconditional and everlasting.
No one will ever be more committed to you than
I am. There is nothing you could ever say or do
that could cause Me to break My commitment to
you. I want you to walk through the rest of your
days feeling secure in Me. You are My chosen one
and My highly valued treasure. I will never leave
you nor forsake you. I am here always and forever.
Take a moment, My precious one, to soak in My
presence. You will hear My still, small voice whisper,
I am near to your heart, now and forever.

Love,
Your committed King

His Leading

My Beloved Daughter,

I love when you allow Me to lead you through this life. I will never force you to yield to Me, however, because I want to give you the freedom to choose whom you will follow. You have nothing to fear if you stay near Me. Remember, I know where you have been and I see where you are going. When times are going well or you want to pursue your own way, you may not feel that you need to hold on to My hand; however, it is unsafe to follow your heart. I am a protective Father who is willing to do whatever it takes to draw you to Myself. Even if you have turned from Me or are in trouble, I am only a prayer away. Your feelings may deceive you, but your faith in Me opens your heart to divine direction and protection. Today I ask, *Will you follow Me, your heavenly Father?*

Love,
Your Lord and Leader

TREASURE OF TRUTH

He is God; we are not!

*Do not forget that he led you through the great
and terrifying wilderness with its poisonous snakes
and scorpions, where it was so hot and dry.
He gave you water from the rock!*

DEUTERONOMY 8:15

143

If you love me,
obey my commandments.

JOHN 14:15

His Commandments

My Beloved,

I am pleased when you obey My commandments.
I established every rule in My Word for your good.
At times you may not understand why I ask you to do
certain things, but they are My ways, not your ways.
You can see only in part, while I see the full scope of
your life and future. You will show your love for Me
by being dedicated to keeping My commandments.
No, you will not be able to follow them perfectly,
and I will not love you more or less because of your
obedience or disobedience. But I will bless you more
and more as you make the hard choices to obey Me.
You never have to worry about the outcome of your
choices if you choose to do all that I ask. There is
never a wrong time to begin obeying Me, so turn to
Me now so I can help you make your wrongs right
and your crooked paths straight!

Love,
Your Father who cherishes you

TREASURE OF TRUTH

Do what is right in God's sight,
and you'll see His blessings begin to flow.

Strength is not seen by how much we can pick up; it is shown by how much we willingly lay down.

Whoever desires to save his life will lose it, but whoever loses his life for My sake will find it. For what profit is it to a man if he gains the whole world, and loses his own soul?

MATTHEW 16:25-26, NKJV

His Life

My Child,

I am the one who gave you life. I formed you in your mother's womb before you were born. I was there when you took your first breath, and I will be there when you take your last one. So live your life for Me. You will never find the true meaning of this life until you willingly lay down your wants, needs, and desires for My sake. If you are willing to lose your life here, you will find the abundant life I offer. If you let go of whatever you hold most tightly, you will find the life your soul is craving. That's because nothing in this world can fill you up the way I can, My beloved. And when you lay down your life, you will not lose anything, but you will gain every good thing I have to offer.

Love,
The Author of your abundant life

His Morals

My Precious Girl,

When you are tempted to compromise your morals and your character, remember that you are Mine. Because I am your Father, your actions are a direct reflection on Me. For that reason, you are called to a higher standard than are those who do not belong to Me. I called you by name and set you apart to bring Me glory. The little things you do with moral excellence will make a difference in how others see Me. It is a privilege to be My child, one you did not have to earn because I chose you. As a member of My heavenly family on earth, I ask you to listen for My voice of conviction. Resolve to walk in integrity every day. When you do, I will lift you up, and you will walk in My favor wherever you go.

Love,
Your perfect King

In view of all this, make every effort to respond to God's promises. Supplement your faith with a generous provision of moral excellence, and moral excellence with knowledge.

2 PETER 1:5

TREASURE OF TRUTH

*It is our character,
not our comfort, that brings
honor to our heavenly
Father.*

His Power

My Daughter,

Don't underestimate the power of My Holy Spirit, who lives in you. He will provide everything you need to be victorious in all areas of your life. When you need a miracle, you can either call on Me or you can call on people who are powerless apart from Me. You can put your faith in humanity or you can put your faith in your heavenly Father, believing I am who I say I am. My power is most evident when I am your only hope. When you have nowhere else to turn, you will witness My mighty hand move in ways you never dreamed possible. I make a way in the wilderness; I part the seas of hopelessness; I rescue My people from the fiery furnace; I pull My children out of prison and put them in a palace. I am your God who will make a way forward when there seems to be no way.

Love,
Your Father of miracles

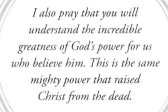

*I also pray that you will
understand the incredible
greatness of God's power for us
who believe him. This is the same
mighty power that raised
Christ from the dead.*

EPHESIANS 1:19-20

His power combined with your faith has no limitations.

For we are not fighting
against flesh-and-blood enemies,
but against evil rulers and authorities
of the unseen world, against mighty powers
in this dark world, and against evil spirits
in the heavenly places.

EPHESIANS 6:12

His Family

My Daughter,

The enemy of your soul wants to divide you against members of your own family. If you're not careful, you will end up falling prey to his plan of attack and wound loved ones. Even if you win the argument, you will lose if you're not fighting for the good of the relationship. Before you engage or entangle yourself in a war you cannot win with words, stop and call out to Me. When you feel anger welling up inside, remember that love is your greatest weapon in any conflict. Because your flesh will fail, you will need to be controlled by the power of My Holy Spirit. Remember you are part of a family—My family. You are on the same team and fighting the same enemy. So fight by doing what is right in My sight, and you will win.

Love,
Your heavenly Father

TREASURE OF TRUTH

We're on the same team, fighting against the same enemy.

His Defense

My Beloved Daughter,

There will be times when people falsely accuse you of something you have not done or said. You will be tempted to defend yourself, but I ask you to allow Me, your heavenly Father, to be your shield. Let truth prevail, and continue to walk in integrity. I don't want you to drain your strength trying to prove your point or ward off an attack. No matter what comes against you, trust Me to defend you. I am a faithful and just God, and no one has more power than I do. My purpose and power in your life will be seen by all if you will be still and let Me fight this battle for you.

Love,
Your heavenly Father and Defender

No weapon forged against you will prevail, and you will refute every tongue that accuses you.

ISAIAH 54:17, NIV

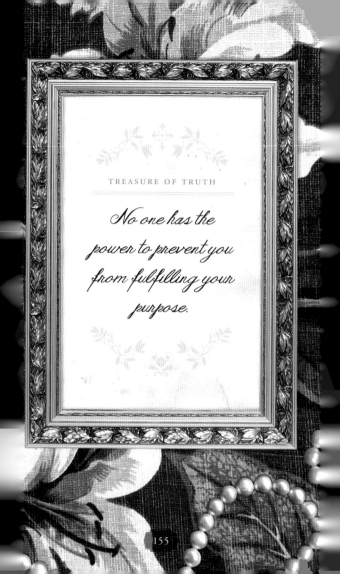

TREASURE OF TRUTH

No one has the power to prevent you from fulfilling your purpose.

TREASURE OF TRUTH

It does not matter what you know if what you know makes no lasting difference.

The people were amazed at his teaching,
for he taught with real authority—quite unlike
the teachers of religious law.

MARK 1:22

156

His Knowledge

My Chosen One,

I love you and long for you to have a deep understanding of who I really am. This world offers many sources of knowledge, but don't value worldly wisdom so much that your vision of who I am becomes confused or clouded. You will come to truly know Me only as you spend time in My Word. As you read, the Holy Spirit will write My truth on the tablet of your heart, and you will be equipped to navigate your way through the trials of this life. So saturate your mind in My Word, and dedicate your life to seeking greater knowledge of Me. Fuel your thoughts with the things of heaven, and find My divine direction in the process. Let Me teach you all you need to know to walk the rest of your days equipped, encouraged, and empowered to do great and mighty works.

Love,
Your wise and holy Father

His Words of Life

My Beloved Daughter,

I have given you the ability to speak words of life, but how you choose to live in front of others will make a much louder statement than what you say. Your loving actions and courageous faith will leave an impact long after any words you speak have been forgotten. You are My representative on this earth, so embrace the opportunity to point others to Me by the way that you love Me. Your actions and reactions toward others will be the key to your witness. My light in you will lead those searching in the dark to Me.

Love,
Your King who shines through you

TREASURE OF TRUTH

His words spoken through you are the difference between a simple conversation and an opportunity for transformation.

I don't speak
on my own authority.
The Father who sent me has
commanded me what to say
and how to say it.

JOHN 12:49

*Having chosen them,
he called them to come to him.
And having called them, he gave
them right standing with himself.
And having given them right
standing, he gave them his glory.*

ROMANS 8:30

TREASURE OF TRUTH

There is no expiration date on God's call for your life!

My Daughter,

I know you want to do something of long-lasting importance. I'm pleased that you want to find your purpose because I have a great calling on your life. I place no expiration date on the call I have for you; no amount of time will cancel what I want to accomplish through you. All I ask is that you tune your ears so you can hear My direction and open your eyes to see where I am leading you. When you make yourself available and quiet yourself enough to hear My call, I will surely direct you onto the path I want you to follow each day.

Love,
Your King who calls to you

My Redeemed One,

You are Mine. If ever you doubt your liberation from sin, look at the Cross and remember My Son's life, which was given for you. I sent Him to set you free forever. All guilt is gone, and you are forgiven. Nothing can hold you back from living a life of freedom in Me—except you. You are set apart and you have been set free, but this victory is yours only if you are willing to walk in it. I love you too much to let you stay weighed down in defeat. Now lay down your shame and let go of the guilt that holds you hostage from the freedom I long to give you. Once you live in My grace, you can share the keys to freedom and forgiveness with others who need to be freed by My mercy. Be My ambassador of hope to a world that is desperately searching for Me!

Love,
Your King, the key to freedom

Guilt chains you to your past;

grace is the key to freedom.

It is for freedom that Christ has set us free.
Stand firm, then, and do not let yourselves be burdened
again by a yoke of slavery.

GALATIANS 5:1, NIV

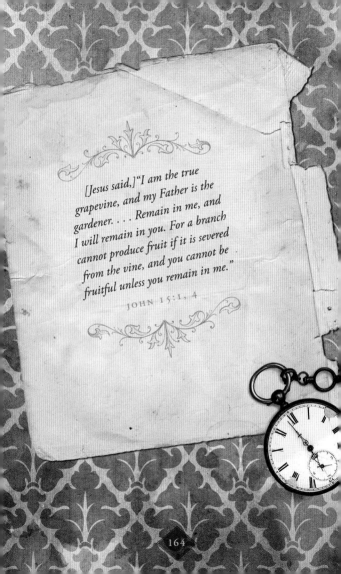

[Jesus said,] "I am the true grapevine, and my Father is the gardener. . . . Remain in me, and I will remain in you. For a branch cannot produce fruit if it is severed from the vine, and you cannot be fruitful unless you remain in me."

JOHN 15:1, 4

His Fruits

My Daughter,

I have chosen you to bear much fruit with your life, but apart from Me you will be powerless and unproductive. No matter how much you love others and want to see them grow, that will not happen apart from Me. My Son is your lifeline and your vine. You are My beautiful branch, and if you will stay connected to Me, My Spirit will flow through you in ways that will bring amazing growth to you and to My Kingdom. Fruit that is seeded by My Holy Spirit will bring a great harvest. When I am the vinedresser, the fruit is sweet and a reflection of all I am in you. There is nothing more delightful than a fruitful life, so stay connected to My vine. Then watch the beautiful fruit that grows from your faithfulness to Me as well as the fruit that bursts forth in the hearts of those you watered with My Word.

Love,
Your God and Vinedresser

TREASURE OF TRUTH

The branches that are most beautiful are those connected to the true Vine . . . Jesus.

*Whatever we treasure
most will be seen in our
attitude and gratitude.*

*Wherever your treasure is,
there the desires of your heart will also be.*

MATTHEW 6:21

166

His Treasure

My Treasured Daughter,

Nothing pleases Me more than when you treasure
your relationship with Me. Ask Me to search your
heart to see what is hidden there. Your heart's desire
will direct every part of your life, My love, and wherever your treasure is, that is where your heart will be
also. Be careful not to put a value on things that will
not last or that do not matter to Me. I am dedicated
to helping you find the treasures that the human eye
cannot see and that no one can take away from you.
I want you to invest in things that will be forever
treasured in heaven. For example, every time you
invest in someone's life for My sake, you are storing
up a precious treasure in heaven. Now is the day to
begin making your eternal investment.

Love,
Your Father who treasures you

His Endurance

My Daughter,

Don't be afraid when your faith is tested. When you feel as if you're in the middle of a raging fire, you may fear that you'll never get out. When you cry out to Me and the blaze continues to burn, you may even wonder if you can continue to trust Me. Never forget that you are not alone; I am with you always. If you feel too weak to keep fighting for your faith, stand firm in what you know to be right and true. I will enable you to persevere, and you will be stronger and more secure in your faith once the flames die down. You will find yourself closer to Me once you've been purified by the fire. This too shall pass, and you will still be standing when it does!

Love,
Your Lord, the source of your endurance

May the Lord lead your hearts into a full understanding and expression of the love of God and the patient endurance that comes from Christ.

2 THESSALONIANS 3:5

TREASURE OF TRUTH

There are a lot of reasons to give up, but there are greater reasons to finish strong.

His Discipline

My Beloved Daughter,

I want you to know that you are treasured, despite any mistake you have made. If you ever feel like you've gone too far, please know I will always make a way for you to come back to Me. It may be hard, but rest assured I will give you as much grace as you need to get back up again. No matter what you do, I will always forgive you when you turn your heart toward Me. I love you and will never walk away from you. However, because of My love, I will discipline you like a father should discipline His daughter. Yes, your wrong choices will lead to consequences. But when you repent, I will run to you with open arms, rejoicing in your return. I am always and forever here for you, My beloved daughter. When you accept My discipline, you will become the woman you long to be and I desire you to become.

Love,
Your faithful Father

*My child,
don't reject the LORD's discipline,
and don't be upset when he corrects
you. For the LORD corrects those
he loves, just as a father corrects
a child in whom he delights.*

PROVERBS 3:11-12

TREASURE OF TRUTH

*Heeding God's correction is much preferable
to continuing in the wrong direction.*

For ever since the world was created,
people have seen the earth and sky.
Through everything God made,
they can clearly see his invisible qualities—
his eternal power and divine nature.
So they have no excuse for not
knowing God.

ROMANS 1:20

His Creation

My Daughter,

I created the heavens and the earth. How I long for you to open your eyes to see everything I've created for you to enjoy. I placed a rainbow in the sky to remind you of My promise. I put stars in the heavens to display My majesty to you. Every evening, I say good night by painting a sunset, and I wake you with the sunrise to brighten and bless your morning. I grow flowers in a rainbow of colors and a bouquet of scents just to see you smile. I don't want you to miss My handiwork because you are worrying about all the circumstances you cannot control. Open your eyes, My beloved, and look around. If you do, you will see Me in new and glorious ways today. And don't forget, of all the things I created . . . you are one of My priceless creations!

Love,
Your heavenly Creator

TREASURE OF TRUTH

Every day God creates a new reminder of His love for you.

His Finish

My Precious Daughter,

When you struggle to let go of sin and shame, My heart breaks as I watch you living with regret and guilt. I sent My Son to purchase your freedom and your salvation. When you cling to Him, nothing you have said or done can hold you hostage. Remember the final words of truth Jesus spoke on the cross: "It is finished." That means anything and everything holding you back from the abundant life I want to give you is vanquished when you repent and accept My forgiveness. The choice is now yours: you can continue to live in what was, or you can choose to let Me set you free. I love you, and I desire for you to give Me whatever you're holding on to today. It is finished, My love!

Love,
The Father and Finisher of your faith

When he had received the drink, Jesus said, "It is finished."
With that, he bowed his head and gave up his spirit.

JOHN 19:30, NIV

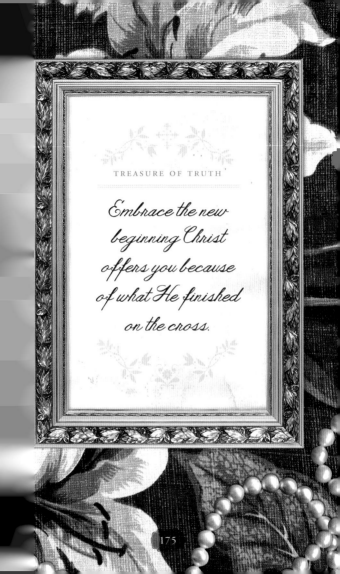

*Embrace the new
beginning Christ
offers you because
of what He finished
on the cross.*

What battle is worth winning on earth if, as a result, you lose souls that could have been won for the Kingdom?

If a kingdom is divided against itself,
that kingdom cannot stand.

MARK 3:24, NIV

176

His Kingdom

My Daughter,

I know some days you feel as if there is no fight left inside of you. You, like all My chosen children, sometimes wonder where I am and whether this faith is worth fighting for. Many times your strength is sapped because you are waging battles I did not ask you to fight. Give up battles not worth winning so you will have the strength to win souls for My Kingdom. I know this life is not easy, but I have not called you to a life of comfort; I have called you to combat and adventure! Battles won for My Kingdom will not be wasted, so ask Me before you choose your fight. I will guide you, and I promise to use you to bring abundant life to all those you love. Now, My beloved daughter, ask yourself, *What am I winning if I lose my chance to glorify my God with my life?*

Love,
Your King who fights for you

MY TREASURE

His Paradise

My Precious Daughter,

Remember that you are not home yet. I know you
don't fully understand now, but the day is approach-
ing when I will come for you and take you to the
beautiful place I have prepared for you. There is
a reason you do not feel at home where you are: I
don't want you to settle into this world. I want you
to settle into Me alone. During this life, you are My
ambassador of love and hope to those who need to
know Me. The time is coming very soon when I will
wipe away every tear you've ever cried, My beloved.
Then you will reign with Me on the new earth I will
create. Let your heart dream of eternity, and let your
soul soar as you breathe in the amazing thought of
being with Me forever.

Love,
Your Dwelling Place

TREASURE OF TRUTH

Don't give up hope; you are not home yet.

No eye has seen, no ear
has heard, and no mind has
imagined what God has
prepared for those
who love him.

1 CORINTHIANS 2:9

A CLOSING THOUGHT FROM

Sheri Rose

I PRAY THAT this book has given you a deeper understanding of how much your heavenly Father loves you, as well as the many treasures that are yours in Christ Jesus. I hope you have also gained a greater appreciation of our God-given privilege to let others know about the riches God wants to offer them!

Though I may never meet you in person, I look forward to meeting you in heaven and celebrating your life lived for an audience of one . . . our Lord.

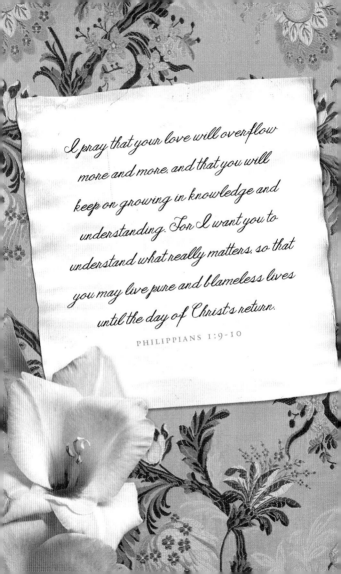

I pray that your love will overflow more and more, and that you will keep on growing in knowledge and understanding. For I want you to understand what really matters, so that you may live pure and blameless lives until the day of Christ's return.

PHILIPPIANS 1:9-10

Acknowledgments

THE MINISTRY WOULD not happen without a team and neither would this book, so I want to thank the following people for what they have invested in me personally and to further God's Kingdom.

First I want to thank my amazing husband, Steven Gene. Thank you for teaching me the Word, for walking with me for twenty-five years, and for covering me in prayer. You are an amazing man, and I am blessed to be your bride. To my beautiful daughter, Emmy Joy, I love traveling and ministering with you. I feel like you're more than just a daughter; I feel like you're my best friend. To my son, Jake, and my beautiful daughter-in-law, Amanda: I am so blessed to have both of you in my life. Thank you for all the God talks and the ways you share your gifts in this ministry. To Julia and Jesse, my amazing and anointed spiritual kids: thank you for serving me so beautifully every day. I also want to thank my gifted and anointed editor, Kim Miller.

Lastly, I want to say thank you to my awesome manager, Jacob Daniel. Steve and I are so honored to have you as part of our family. You are such a gifted and godly young man. There are no words to express my deep appreciation for the endless hours you work, the Bible studies you direct, and the way you lay down your comfort every day to go to combat for God's Kingdom. Only on the other side of eternity will you see the many lives that were touched because you chose to use your gifts for the glory of God and not yourself.

In Christ,
Sheri Rose

also from
SHERI ROSE SHEPHERD

YOUR HEART'S DESIRE
*DVD Group Experience
also available*

IF YOU HAVE A CRAVING,
I HAVE A CURE

MY BEAUTIFUL PRINCESS BIBLE

BOOKING REQUESTS

For more information about *His Treasure*, including
how to schedule a His Treasure conference or retreat
weekend with Sheri Rose, e-mail her directly at
rose@biblelifecoaching.com or e-mail jacob@biblelifecoaching.com.
And be sure to visit her website: **www.biblelifecoaching.com.**

CP0673

SHERI ROSE SHEPHERD is an award-winning author, Bible life coach, and humorist with over one million books sold. Her life experiences help her identify with almost any woman's battle. She grew up in a broken home and was severely overweight as a teen; she also experienced depression, dyslexia, and an eating disorder. Through God's strength, Sheri Rose has become a bestselling author and popular speaker at events nationwide, including Women of Joy and Extraordinary Women. Her weekly video devotions are featured on Bible Gateway. Visit her online at www.biblelifecoaching.com and on Facebook at www.facebook.com/biblelifecoaching.